ARCHAIC TRACKS ROUND CAMBRIDGE

ALFRED WATKINS

Written by Alfred Watkins (1855–1935)

First published in 1932

This edition © 2021 by Heritage Hunter

Available in paperback and ebook formats.

Cover image: Runway Perspective by Eric Ravilious (1903–1942)

Also available from Heritage Hunter:

The Old Straight Track by Alfred Watkins

The Ley Hunter's Manual by Alfred Watkins

Available from Amazon and **www.heritagehunter.co.uk**

Free weekly *Histories* newsletter, **www.gethistories.com**

CONTENTS

Introduction   vii

1. A BASIS FOR INVESTIGATION   1
2. ACCIDENTAL COINCIDENCE   8
3. CAMBRIDGE BOROUGH MAP   10
4. CAMBRIDGE DISTRICT MAP   14
5. PRE-HISTORIC ORIGIN OF GREAT ROADS   21
6. SEASONAL ALINEMENTS   30
7. CARDINAL-POINT ALINEMENTS   38
8. PLACE-NAMES   53
9. CONFIRMATION AND MORE TRACKS   57
10. NOTES   64

Appendix A   71
Appendix B   73

"To guide my course aright,
What mound or steady mere is
 offered to my sight."

…

(Mountains and hills are
 declaiming)

"Besides, we are the marks, which
 looking from on high,
The traveller beholds; and with a
 cheerful eye
Doth thereby shape his course, and
 freshly doth pursue
The way which long before lay
 tedious in his view."

—

MICHAEL DRAYTON (*POLYOLBION*, SONGS FIRST AND SEVENTH).

INTRODUCTION

Herein is a framework for local and field investigation, a prima facie case, for of the two equally important branches of enquiry—map and field work—I offer the first only. I leave the field work to those who by health-giving tramps along the lines indicated, will, I feel sure, find new corroboration.

A flying visit to Cambridge, and a glance at local maps showed the district to be unusually rich in mark-point evidence, and two mornings scouting round Cambridge Castle gave the probable limits of the pre-Roman camp there.

I keep to evidence more than conclusions. Two questions naturally arise: "When was this done ?" and "What race of men did this skilled work?" I make no attempt to answer here.

The multiplicity of crossing tracks will clash with the preconceptions of most readers. But why not? In primitive days, when no property rights stood in the way, a path was easily started by the instinctive way of walking for a mark on the sky-line. "The number of the people is countless, and their dwellings exceedingly numerous," testifies Cæsar. It is natural that tracks should be thicker on the ground than to-day.

With baited breath I suggest that the official attitude which allows the planning of a sighted track and its mounds, but limits the knowledge to one nation only—the Romans—is weak, in face of the records in the Old Testament. For there, five hundred years before Rome was a nation, it is clear that prophets and chroniclers were perfectly familiar with "Straight paths for your feet," with all their attributes of "waymarks," "high heaps," "standards," "beacons," and "high places." "Let your eyes look straight on" was the instruction, and the tracks were even then "ancient paths" in danger of degenerating into "crooked ways." The Romans learnt it all from earlier races, and so might well the Celtic races in Britain.

John Bunyan, too, who, as a tinker, travelled this very country, was quite sure about the "narrow way," "as straight as a rule can make it, cast up by the patriarchs, the prophets, Christ and his apostles." This from his beloved Bible, but the stone causeway through the morass he did not find there, but in his own native and watery land, with just such straight causeways as he pictures.

If the reader finds me packing too much detail in these covers, can he not just dip into it—as he would into a dictionary, for only that place, district or "lay of the land" in which he is interested?

Lacking local knowledge, I shall make blunders, as accepting for mark-point a site not ancient. But if several examples are spoilt by such weakness, I must remind logical readers that half-a-dozen fully proved sighted tracks of pre-Roman date across country are sufficient for proof that such a system was here before the Romans came.

Before condemning any connection between archaic tracks and sun observation, consider the pertinent evidence I give in Chapter VI. of a Welsh word indicating that "a slight track or path" was habitually made by astronomers with the aid of light observation.

A. W.
5, Harley Court,
Hereford.

1
A BASIS FOR INVESTIGATION

I do not begin with a conclusion, but no pioneer ever worked with a blank mind, and the framework for this enquiry is something as follows:

That early man, sighting his way across country from or to hill-points, laid down as guide-marks for his fellows, in that straight line which was decided with the edict "Let there be light," a line of sight-marks.

These, mounds or tumuli, moats or moated mounds, unusual-looking unworked stones, and hill-notches.

That these marks, like the "high places" of the Old Testament, became gathering points for an expanding civilization. That at many of them are now churches, castles, and ancient homesteads.

That blended with the alinement system fixing such man-made sites, came alinements to sunrise or sunset, cross-country dials to give seasonal information.

That beacon-lights, associated with special seasons, were used in conjunction with an organised plan, of which much record remains in place-names, in folk-lore, in old customs, and even in children's games.

The above framework, like the scaffolding of a huge building, was not there at the beginning of my enquiry, but has grown with accumulated evidence.

MOUNDS

Mounds (tumuli) are dateable archæologically. If they aline on a straight track established by evidence beyond possibility of accidental coincidence, the track must be at least as old as the mound. A "commanding position" on a ridge or hill (so often noted) confirms their use as sight marks, and their proved use for burials does not clash with a dual primary purpose as a sighting-mark. They are the one great means of dating tracks.

I have to adopt a view concerning the great mound of Cambridge Castle, which is at variance with most authorities. I see ample proof that it existed (perhaps as a mound of smaller size), on its present site in prehistoric times, long before any Normans came. It is obvious that the straight line of the Huntingdon Road (No. 2), was laid out by sighting on the mound, which was therefore there at least as early as the track. Those present-day authorities, who assume that this and other straight roads were engineered in the Roman period, are on the horns of a dilemma, for they also assume. that the mound, which they classify as a "Norman Motte" was not there when the Normans landed. No. 19 also shows the Chesterton Road to be alined on the mound for a distance. I devote a chapter in The Old Straight Track to the ample evidence that all over Britain the Castle mounds .now classified as "Norman Mottes" belong to an earlier period. In many cases there are traces of a mound having also existed at the knuckle-corner of the vallum of a camp or castle, and that tracks aline to this. Pleasant Hill is an instance of this.

MOATS

While a few moats may be entirely mediæval, the majority, I feel sure, originate from a prehistoric moated enclosure, perhaps akin to an island in a small lake, or a moated flat mound.

CHURCHES

These are a stumbling block to objectors, as the origin of the building is clearly later than prehistoric times. But the evidence that practically all ancient ones are built on "Pagan Sites" is overwhelming.

Mr. Walter Johnson, in his *Byways in Archæology*, devotes a long chapter to this, and I do the same in *The Old Straight Track*. Plentiful evidence in the Bible shows the continuity—chiefly on "high places"—of such sites from paganism to Christianity. In No. 13 alinement, five churches are precisely in line within sixteen miles; there is only one church in each parish, so it seems beyond a possibility of accidental coincidences, especially as there is evidence of a man-made alinement in the fact that it is precisely east and west.

MARK-STONES

In my own western border-land, a few ancient stones are marked on the map, but for each one of these I find by field-survey four or five others. In the Cambridge maps I find none marked. I have not the slightest doubt that some are to be found if looked for, even in the towns and large villages. They can often be found on a track followed up on foot, and Mr. W. A. Dutt (who wrote a pamphlet on the Mark-stones of East Anglia) reports instances of this.

CROSS-ROADS

The crossing-point of two ancient tracks seems often to continue as a cross-road of present day, even when the rest of the old track has vanished. Where a cross-road comes into alinement it is corroboration, not counting so highly as say a mound, but if it has an ancient place-name, or is crossed by a second alinement, it counts as a good point. Road-junctions have a similar value, counting, say, as half-points.

HILL-NOTCHES

These—formed by a track being cut deeply on a bank—are common in hilly districts, and may be found by frequent examination of the skyline. The notch can only be seen when standing in the right alinement. Crackhow Farm indicates one, somewhere near, or in view of, its site. "Nick," "Scar," and

"Bwlch" (the Welsh form) are other names for hill-notches.

STRAIGHT ROADS

These are exceedingly plentiful in this rather flat district, and probably most of them are comparatively modern. After all, the nearest way between two places is a straight line. The most unsafe way to look for ancient tracks is to extend present straight ones; the right way is to see whether a sufficient number of good mark-points (mounds, stones, &c.) aline. Then if a bit of straight road falls on the line, it is extra proof. But still, on this map, as other chapters will show, a good many straight bits of present road have good mark-points beyond their ends, and are therefore proved to be on ancient tracks.

CAMPS

Continued map and field work on numerous camps (not in this district) has shown close relations between tracks and camps, the latter having clearly originated where the interspaces between crossing tracks occur on high ground. It is impracticable to do real work on camps without the 6-inch Ord. maps, and except for Cambridge Borough, I have consulted none for this district. So investigation remains to be done.

The straight archaic tracks usually touch the edges of camps they approach. This is fully illustrated in the *Ley Hunter's Manual*.

The two Arbury Camps, the almost destroyed camp

at Cambridge, one above Great Shelford, and Vandlebury Camp, are thus outlined in my plans.

Another example, not marked on the plans, can be found by a line through Boxworth Church, Knapwell Church, and Coldharbour Farm, as between the churches it falls on the vallum (earthen walls) of a small camp. Unrecorded camps will often be discovered by the alinements in this way.

Vandlebury Camp seems to have evolved (it is an exceptional case), from a stone circle, for in addition to one track edging it, I found, unexpectedly, two others going through its centre.

TRACKS OUT OF SIGHT

All original archaic tracks are now out of sight, buried a foot or two below the surface. Darwin has demonstrated how the earthworms have seen to that, the rate of raising the earth surface being somewhere about an inch each century. So the old tracks have to be dug for to be seen. I find them from 18 inches to two feet below the surface, deeper in river-flood areas, and far less on open hills. At the Queen Stone in a Wye meadow, the Bronze Age surface was at least three feet below the present.

Even if a straight footpath is now on the old site it is an overlay, and the same with surviving bits of modern roads seen in my maps on the lines. Roman roads were so splendidly engineered that even if out of use they survive and can be traced, but more feeble tracks disappear quickly. These facts are the reasons why the surviving mark-points are the means of detection.

Writers on topography seem all to have fallen into the error of regarding those tracks now to be partially or faintly seen on the land as being the earliest organised ones, thus going back only hundreds, instead of thousands, of years.

Natural human needs led (at some period) to paths along high ridges, and the fact of pre-historic mounds being often grouped along the same positions has been wrongly interpreted as proving the antiquity of Ridgeways. But the mounds were not mark-points for these, but for older tracks crossing the hill. A present-day track naturally runs along the Malvern Hill ridge, and alongside it are a couple of tumuli. Standing on one of these I have seen in the Worcester plain below two separate lengths of converging road alining to the mound. These are on sites of tracks far earlier than the ridgeway.

2

ACCIDENTAL COINCIDENCE

Critics say—and with some show of reason—"Look at the large number of 'ancient sites,' peppered all over your map. Alinements such as you get through a number of points can easily come by accidental coincidence, not proving the lines to be man-made."

It is well to face this argument, for I have sometimes found advocates of my thesis quoting instances which either have too few mark-points for real proof, or are too careless in the accuracy of alinement.

As regards the last point, I ought to mention that before inking in the rather coarse lines on the sketch-maps, the greatest possible care was taken to see that the lines, put in first with a fine lead pencil and a long accurate straight edge, do go precisely through the mark-points on the map, with no error. To be "near," as for instance the corner of the churchyard when taking a church as mark-point is not acceptable.

Assuming this standard of accuracy, I have marked

haphazard a number of crosses with pencil on a sheet of paper to see how many alinements can be found.

Beginning with a three-point alinement, this was found to have no value as evidence of human arrangement, for an average of one such line comes when only nine marks are made on a sheet, and with a hundred mark-points there were at least as many three-point alinements as points.

But the case is quite different if a four-point alinement is looked for, only one or two instances being discoverable on a large sheet with a hundred points. It was then found that the chances of a five-point alinement are still scarcer, and this in geometric proportion, for many trial sheets can be made without finding one.

I, therefore, take five-points as my minimum standard for a fair (but not an absolute) presumption of proof. When such a map-alinement is found there almost invariably follows convincing evidence with field-survey, additional mark-stones, bits of ancient tracks, hill-notches, legends of underground passages on the line, or other items.

All my plans in this book had the ancient sites or mark-points marked in exact position as on the Ordnance maps; this was done before the lines were ruled through these points. The lines were *not* ruled first and the sites planted on them. All are maps (although reduced), not theoretic sketch-diagrams.

3

CAMBRIDGE BOROUGH MAP

This is based on a larger scale than the subsequent maps, and in order to bring in outside confirming mark-points the dotted lines indicating such extension are not to the same scale, the distances being marked.

The following are the seven tracks or alinements:—

1. Coldharbour Farm—Scotland Farm—Two miles of the Maddingley Road (this although undulating obviously based on a slight line)—Magdelene or Great Bridge over the Cam—Triangulation point on Butt Green—On present footpath through Coldham Common—Six-Mile-Bottom Cross-roads.

2. Fen Stanton Church (on adjoining Ord. map)—On 4½ miles of Huntingdon Road or VIA DEVANA—Site marked for ancient Cemetery in Girton College grounds—Great Mound of Cambridge Castle.

. . .

3. Long Stanton (All Saints) Church—A mile of straight road—Eastern vallum of Cambridge Castle Camp—St. Clements Church—The Round Church—Petty Cury cross-roads—On a full mile of main streets and part of the Hills Road.

4. Belsars Hill Camp (adjoining map)—(Woodhouse Farm)—Pleasant Hill (corner mound of Cambridge Camp)—Mill Pit and footpath—Great Shelford Church—Strethall Church.

5. Roman Camp. S. of Ely (on adjoining map)—On two miles of Akeman Street (adjoining map)—after a gap, on another two and a half miles of the site of Akeman Street—Pleasant Hill, site of mound—(Leckhampton House)—Barrington Church.

6. Milton Moat—Chesterton Moat—Petty Cury cross-roads—Mill Pit and two boundary Stones beyond it—Haslingfield Church—Tumulus below Morden Grange.

7. Half-a-mile of road at Horningsea—Horningsea Church—Chesterton Moat—Across Midsummer Common over present site of Victoria Bridge—St.

Clement's Church (oriented at the angle)—Barton Moat and Church—Thorn Hill.

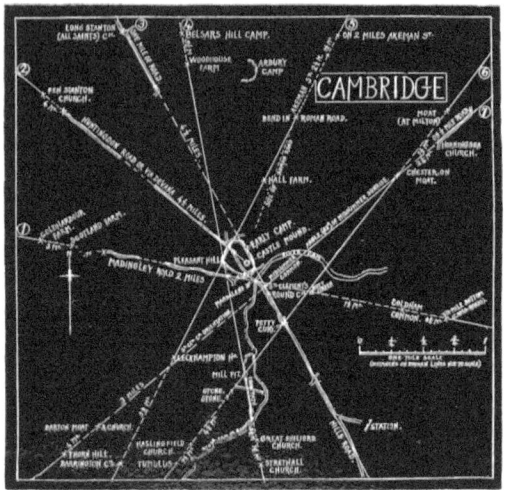

PLAN I.   CAMBRIDGE BOROUGH (large scale).

I expect that those with a local knowledge of ancient town sites of chapels and churches will find corroboration in these. And it is, I think, likely that ancient mark-stones might be found if looked for. No. 2 is apparently a Midsummer Sunset line (see Admiral Boyle Somerville's table in Appendix), and No. 7 one for Midsummer Sunrise, this last confirmed by the name of the Common and by the orientation to the line of St. Clements Church. Numbers 9, 14, and 19 in the next map and chapter, ought to have been marked in this one, but were discovered too late.

CAMBRIDGE DISTRICT.

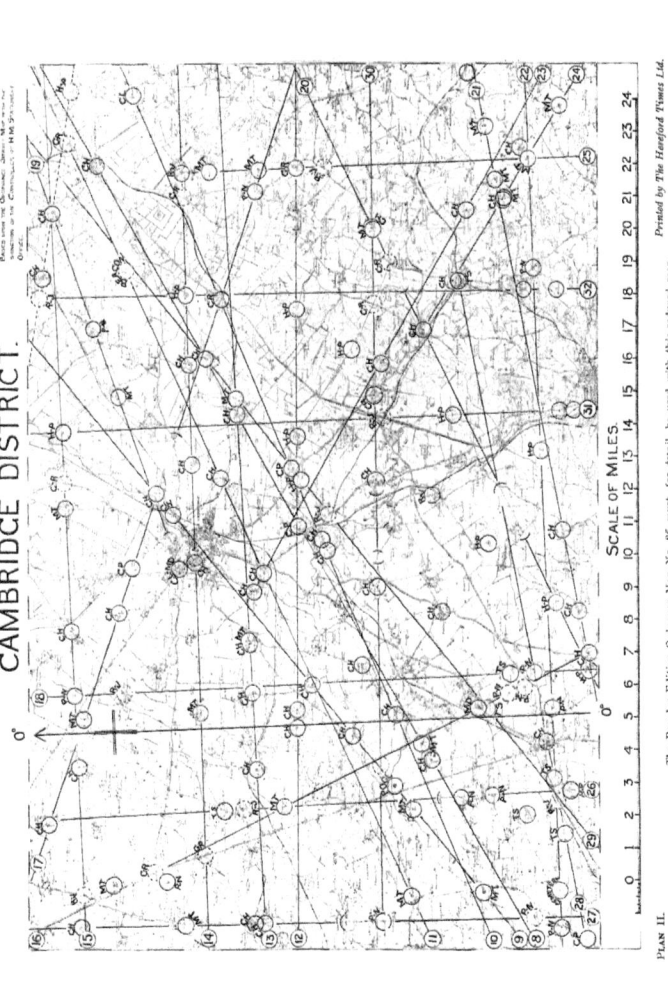

PLAN II.   The Popular Edition Ordnance Map No. 85 must, for detail, be used with this reduced map.   *Printed by The Hertford Times Ltd.*

4
CAMBRIDGE DISTRICT MAP

The cardinal-point alinements are marked "Grid."

8. Whaddon Church—Hoback Farm Moat—Harston road-junction—Camp north of Shelford—Fulbourn Church—Great Wilbraham Church—Church in Newmarket.

9. Moat near Guilden Morden—Wendy Moat—Wimpole circular pond—Orwell Church—Harlton Church—On part of Newmarket Road, Cambridge—Barnwell ancient Chapel—Fen Ditton Church.

10. Ancient Church, Malton Farm—Little Shelford Church—Great Shelford Church—Centre of Vandlebury Camp—Six-Mile-Bottom cross roads—(Hill House Farm) —Cheveley Castle.

. . .

11. Tadlow Moat—(Fox Hill)—Trumpington Church—Cherry Hinton Church—Beacon Farm—On two miles of Icknield Way.

12. Great Eversden Church—Little Eversden Church—N. vallum of Shelford Camp—Tumulus on Copley Hill—The Tower, 348ft.—Bit of road at Weston Colville—Cross-roads and Church at Carlton.

13 (*Grid*). Little Gransden Church—Kingston Church—Comberton Church—Barton Church—Fulbourn Church—Fulbourn Moat.

14 (*Grid*). Caxton Gibbet cross-roads—Hardwick Moat—Great St. Mary's Church and Market Hill, Cambridge—Petty Cury cross-roads—Teversham Church—Little Wilbraham Churchyard (north side)—Centre of the circular enclosure of Allington Hill—Five-ways crossroads at Stetchworth—Stetchworth village road-junction.

15 (*Grid*). Road-junction, Papworth—Boxworth Church—Noon Folly Farm—Oakington Church—Landbeach Moat—Cross-roads, Waterbeach.

. . .

16. Four Miles of Ermine Street, ending at Caxton Gibbet—Kingston Wood Moat—(Field Barn)—Melbourn Bury—Munsey Farm—Barley Church.

17. Conington Church—Moat at Lolworth—Girton Church—Arbury Camp—2¼ miles of Fleam Dyke—Six-Mile-Bottom cross-roads—The Chantry.

18 (*Grid*). Noon Folly Farm, Lolworth—Goffer's Knoll—Noon's Folly Farm, Royston—High point near Barley.

19. Exning Church—The Abbey, Staffham Prior—Anglesea Abbey—On a mile of Chesterton Road—Great Mound of Cambridge Castle.

20. West Wickham Moat—Mark's Grave cross-roads—Field path for ¾ mile—Linton Church—1½ miles of straight road—Chishall Down Hill-point, 451ft.—Hill-point near Barley.

21. Church at Sturmer Hall—Moat at Horsham Hall—326ft. Hill-point, Ashton—Elmdon Church—Cross-roads, Chrishall—Great Chishall Church.

. . .

22 (*Grid*). Stream-crossing at Steeple Bumpstead—Helion Moat—Goldstones—Heavy Hill, 331ft.—Burloes (ancient burials at this hill-farm)—Tumuli, Thursfield Down—Site of ancient Cemetery—The Bury, Ashwell.

23. Shudy Camps Church—Hildersham Church—Half-mile of field road—Trumpington Church—Grandchester Church.

24. Latchley's Farm Moat—Helion Moat—Castle Camps Moat—Castle Camps Church—Bartlow Church—Linton Church.

25 (*Grid*). Helion Moat—Road-junction, Carlton Green—Cross-roads and Church, Carlton—Moat below Burrough Green—Moat—One-third-mile village road at Stetchworth, and road-junction.

26 (*Grid*). 420 hill-point, Pen Hills—South End and ¼ mile of road, Bassinbourn—North End and ¾ mile of field road, Bassinbourn—Kingston Wood Moat—Road-junction, Bourn—Tumulus N. of Bourn.

27 (*Grid*). Cold Harbour—Hatley Gate—1¼ miles of track—Little Gransden Church—Great Gransden

Church—Moat below Eltesley—Papworth St. Agnes Church.

28. North Edge of Arbury Camp—Tumulus near Morden Grange—Two tumuli—Royston Church—On two miles of Icknield Way—Noon's Folly Point—Tumulus on Bartlow Hills.

29. Tumulus at Melbourn—Little Trees Hill—centre of Vandlebury Camp—Moat at Fulbourn—Great Wilbraham Church.

30 (*Grid*). Hatley Gate—Hoback Farm—Newton Church—On a "dog's leg" in a road near Newton—On ¼ mile of road at Sawston—Sawston Church—Little Abington Church—West Wickham Church.

31 (*Grid*). Bridge-crossing of river Cam—Northend place and bit of road—326 hill-point near Park Farm—Cross-roads (a nodal-point) near Pampisford Station—North Hills, a farm-homestead.

32 (*Grid*). Mortimers—Ashdon Church—Centre of Allington Hill—Tumulus 4/10ths mile N. of Hill—Road-Gap in Devils Dyke—Road-junction near Burwell. (Also confirmed by going through crossing-points of other

alinements at 12 mile-stone near Linton, and in Borden Wood.)

SOME CHARACTERISTICS

Nos. 8, 9, 23, and 30 are four-church alinements with other good mark-points.

No. 13 is a five-church alinement, with another good mark-point, a moat.

Nos. 11, 12, 17, 19, 20, 22, 23, 25, 26, 27, 28, and 30 all have straight bits of lengths or present-day road or track on the line, these surviving fragments of the original track.

The only "Beacon" place-name has a track (No. 11) through it. It is probable that the name does not signify an actual fire-beacon at this spot, but that the place was alined to a beacon.

Great Shelford and Little Shelford; Great Gransden and Little Gransden; and Great Eversden and Little Eversden are churches respectively linked up by track alinements.

Although farms are often ancient sites and good mark-points for tracks, they have not been ringed and accepted as such except in a few cases with convincing ancient place-names. Noon Folly and Hoback Farms were confirmed by two tracks alining through them.

"Goldstones" in its name indicated ancient mark-stones, and this was confirmed by two distinct tracks coming through the spot.

Convincing fragments of confirmation came in drawing up the map when bits of present day road seem to come out of their way to shape themselves to the old track. This is seen in the dog-leg on No. 30, and the curious straight fragment at Weston Colville in No. 20.

Most convincing of all were the cases where two distinct tracks, each indicated by a string of mark-points, found their way to an evidently commanding hill-point, marked on the Ord. map with its height. This occurred to Chrishall Down, 451ft., Pen Hills, 420 ft., and a 298ft. point near the lower VIA DEVANA.

GRID OF CARDINAL-POINT ALINEMENTS

This is made up of the following Nos.:—
    North and South: Nos. 27, 26, 18, 31, 32 and 25.
    East and West: Nos. 15, 14, 13, 30 and 22.

5
PRE-HISTORIC ORIGIN OF GREAT ROADS

Of the old roads of Britain the four mentioned in the "Laws of Edward the Confessor" are the theme of many who write on the subject. They are: "Watlinge strete, Fosse, Hikenilde strete, and Erminge strete." To these may be added other famous ones, as Stane Street, Akeman Street, Sarn Helen (chiefly in Wales), Via Julia, Via Devana, Peddar's Way, and The Pilgrim's Way.

My investigation into such roads is not to decide what clan of men made them or when, but to investigate their evolution, and whether the usual assumption that each one was a distinct separately made organisation has any foundation, for there is no doubt that some of these names (as Stane or Stone), are generic ones applied to several roads.

There happen to be in this map stretches of four of the above roads, namely, Ermine Street, Icknield Way, Akeman Street, and Via Devana, and also a local one named Ashwell Street.

It must not be assumed that the marking of these names on the map indicates the real course of the historic "Way," and an open mind should be kept as to whether their origin was not that of a selected route over a great number of pre-existing tracks, which route being stoned and made efficient for more and more traffic, outlived the lighter trails from which it was formed and has in parts survived for us to see, when all the rest has gone underground.

The feature common to all, is that they run in straight courses, seldom of great length, but in sections at slight angles to each other, and lengths varying (in this map), from less than a mile to the 13½ miles of Ermine street. Obviously these straight sections were originally laid down by a sighting method, for no rule or stretched cord can be laid down on uneven land for such lengths.

To sight such lines across country, a terminal elevated point, either natural or artificial is required. By a study of such mark-points in alinements we can judge whether each section was made as part of one continuous whole— in which case you would expect to find one only sighting knoll in line, and that one near the nodal point or angle— or whether each section was not part of an older track now vanished—in which case you would expect to find a line of mark-points beyond the nodal or angle of the named road being investigated, with occasionally fragments of surviving track.

This is what I investigate, and here give a digest of such branch extensions of the four named roads. I found it necessary to do this on two plates to avoid confusion with the close proximity of crossing tracks. Note that the Street names are used as labels only, for bits so marked on the map, not as endorsing the map-maker's guess that these bits were actually part of an original great road.

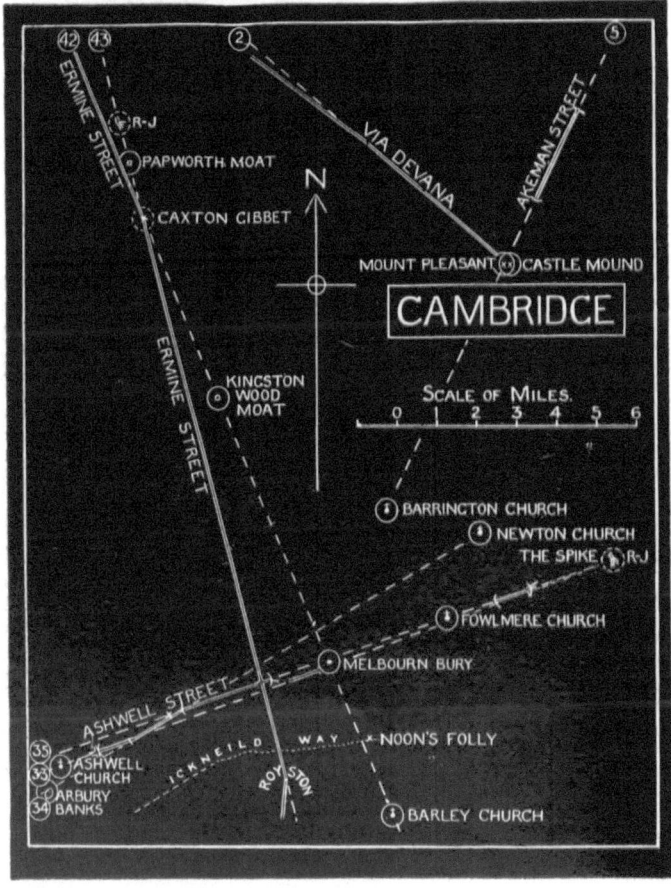

PLAN III.   ORIGIN OF ERMINE STREET, &c.

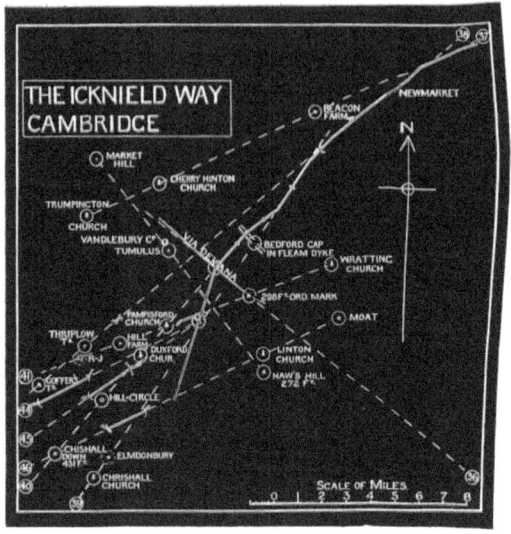

PLAN IV.   ORIGIN OF ICKNIELD WAY.

ASHWELL STREET (Plan III.)

33. Ashwell Church—One mile of Ashwell Street past High Town Farm—A mile of field-track west of Melbourn—"The Spike" road-junction.

34. North edge of Arbury Banks—1¼ miles of Ashwell Street—Newton Church. This track is sighted on one of the three low hills, West Hill, Cockle Hill, or Clunch Pitt Hill, all on the line.

35. Site of "Cemetery" south of Littleton—Two miles of Ashwell Street—Foulmere Church—Three-quarter mile

of straight field-road beyond Thirplow—"The Spike" road-junction.

VIA DEVANA. (Plan III.)

2. (This on Cambridge Borough Map). Fen Stanton Church—4½ miles of Via Devana—Cambridge Castle Mound; no track beyond here.

36 (Plan IV.) Boxworth Church—Half-a-mile of straight road at Dry Drayton—Wrangling Corner—One-and-a-half miles of Via Devana past Worsted Lodge—298ft. Ord. Triangulation Point. (A present road goes on as far as Marks Grave, but does not seem to be sighted).

AKEMAN STREET. (Plan III.)

5. Roman Camp S. of Ely—Two miles of Akeman Street (foregoing on the adjoining Ely map)—(Gap of 1½ miles) —Two-and-a-half miles of Akeman Street—Bordering Cambridge Castle Camp—Pleasant Hill Mound—Barrington Church.

ICKNIELD STREET. (Plan IV.)

37. Two miles of Icknield Way to Thetford Road junction north of Newmarket—Beacon Farm—Cherry Hinton Church—Trumpington Church—Tadlow Moat.

. . .

38. Two miles of Icknield Way (past Heath Stud Farm)—Short field-road—Road-junction—Road through Whittlesford—Thirplow tumulus—Goffer's Knoll.

39. Three miles of Icknield Way past Six-Mile-Bottom—Through Fleam Dyke at Bedford Gap—Elmdonbury (ancient site)—Chrishall Church.

40. Two miles of Icknield Way north of Worsted Lodge—Road-junction at Duxford—Circular Enclosure Hill-point—Chishall Down, a Hill-point of 451 feet, 10 miles from Icknield Way, but evidently the sighting point for this section.

41. West Wratting Church—298ft. Triangulation-point (same as No. 34 is sighted on)—One mile of a present-day road—Pampisford Church—(Hill Farm)—Road-junction, Thirplow—Tumulus at Melbourn—Limlow Hill with tumulus, 220 feet.

ERMINE STREET. (Plan III.)

42. Four Miles straight of Ermine Street down to Caxton Gibbet—Kingston Wood Moat—(Field Barn)—Melbourn Bury (earthwork)—(Munsey Farm)—Half-a-mile of road—Barley Church.

. . .

43. Road-junction east of Papworth St. Agnes—Moat east of Papworth Everard—Thirteen and a half miles of Ermine Street from Caxton Gibbet through Royston.

Here follow some apparent connections with Icknield Way.(Plan IV.)

44. Road-junction near Pampisford Station—2¼ miles of straight road—Cross-road at Coach and Horses—Heath Farm Moat—420ft. point on Pen Hills.

45. Road-junction near Pampisford Station—Duxford Church—Two miles of straight road.

46. West Wickham Moat—Mark's Grave Cross-roads—Linton Church—(crosses Icknield Way)—One-and-a-half miles of straight road—Chishall Down, 451ft.

I present these two sketch maps for local investigation, and leave exact deductions to others. Sighting methods are certainly used, for almost all the roads are in lengths of straight lines. Note what a hotch-potch of eratic course, not necessitated by uneven ground, is for instance the Icknield Way from Newmarket downwards. How can such a route be explained unless parts of many previously planned roads had to be made use of?—an expediency method we adopt now, and have done for centuries.

Note the abundant evidence of road-alinements having once run far beyond their present use in these supposed trunk roads. And in some cases (33, 35, 38, 41, 42) fragments of remaining tracks confirm this.

The way in which the track-alinements (indicated first by other mark points), fall precisely on well-known hill-points with altitudes marked on the Ord. map, is most convincing as to the use of long-distance sighting methods. Goffer's Knoll, Chishall Down, 420 point on Pen Hills, and Limlow Hill are instances, all but the last-named actually having two different tracks in my maps sighted on them.

The complicated question how the Icknield Way (if correctly marked as coming through Royston), is joined up to the well-marked course coming through Newmarket, is perhaps answered by one or other of the three straight bits in alinements Nos. 44, 45, 46. Of these, two, Nos. 44, 45, radiate from a point on the Way itself, and it looks as if they might have been sighted in connection with it, and therefore not (in this case) older. The other is sighted on a distant hill.

I think (from the evidence) that a certain proportion of the straight pieces of roads which from their surface structure are known to be Roman, were really planned and sighted on then new sites by the Romans. These, I surmise, links necessary to join up the ancient straight tracks which they were adopting and reconstructing.

There is room for exhaustive study as to which of the

mounds are Roman in their origin, and whether these also aline on straight tracks. Despite the official maps of Roman Roads, our knowledge on these points is—chaos.

6
SEASONAL ALINEMENTS

Primitive man, after he began to cultivate the land, had need for marking the year's progress to aid him in deciding when to prepare the land, and when to sow.

So a division into four quarters was evolved by the wise-men, and fire and other festivals organised, which still survive in folk-lore, dates of fairs and feasts, saints' days and religious festivals.

The first system in Britain, although observation of sun-rise was obviously required, was based on the crop needs.

THE CELTIC VEGETATION YEAR

- First Quarter-day (Brid—St. Bridget—Candlemas), Feb. 1—4.
- Second Quarter-day (Beltaine—May Day), May 1—6.
- Third Quarter-day (Lugh or Lug—Lammas), Aug. 1—8.

- Fourth Quarter-day (Samhain—Martinmas—Mayor chosen), Nov. 1—8.

The second date is that given by Lockyer, but it varied between that and the first of the month at different times.

As the sun really decided these dates, the wise-men, as their knowledge advanced, soon brought in another yearly division, openly based on sun observations, also divided into quarters.

THE SUN OR JUNE YEAR

- First Quarter-day (Shortest day—Mid-Winter—Christmas), Dec. 25—23.
- Second Quarter-day (Equal day and night—Lady Day), Mar. 25—21.
- Third Quarter-day (Longest day—Midsummer—St. John's), June 24—21.
- Fourth Quarter-day (Equal day and night—Michaelmas), Sept. 24—23.

But the provision of this more correct astronomical year division did not supersede the older cultivation-year, the use of which still lingers, as in the perplexity of one tenancy commencing on Candlemas day (Feb. 2) and another on Lady Day (Mar. 25). The second figure in above table is the correct astronomical division as given by Lockyer. The first the modern deviation.

These two tables together divide the sun-year (based on the solstices and equinoxes) into eight fairly accurate divisions.

Skilled observers, as Mr. A. L. Lewis, Sir Norman Lockyer, and Admiral Boyle Somerville, have demonstrated the fact that in our British megalithic monuments (stone circles and dolmens), there is strong evidence of alinements to sunrise and sunset on these seasonal periods. This evidently for calendar fixing.

I have found, and demonstrated in my books, that many similar alinements are not merely within sight of the stones of a monument, but extend over mark-points for miles across country. Place-names, legends, and church-orientation also confirm this.

Alinement No. 7 in Chapter 3 seems to be to Midsummer sunrise, and this is not only confirmed by its passing through Midsummer Common, but by the church of St. Clement's through which it passes being oriented the same.

I have no doubt that other alinements in my plans are seasonal, but as the aim of this book is not a full exposition, but data for local observation and enquiry, I do not dwell on the facts of sun observations, customs and practices, nor on the use of beacon-fires in connection. In addition to No. 7, Nos. 9, 29, and 38 may possibly be to Midsummer sunrise.

A study of Frazer's *Golden Bough*, of Lockyer's *Stonehenge*, and of Admiral Boyle's Somerville's papers in *Archæologia*, Vol. XXIII., will give the basis. As it is not well to encumber this chapter with the rather profuse tables of figures which will aid working students, they will be found as Appendices A. and B.

Because the glib phrase "Sun Worship" is constantly used by most writers, including experts, I must protest that students should not assume any such fact in Britain, where I have seen no sound evidence for it. Even if sun observation became a ritual performed at stated seasons, there is strong evidence that the purport was utilitarian.

The early Christian missionaries no doubt condemned all ritual practices which preceded their own purer religion, in the same way as King Canute did later in a law against "The barbarious worship of stones, trees, fountains, and of the heavenly bodies." This however was probably the ignorant prejudice of non-British men brought up in old traditions of races who really did worship many gods. If they had seen the captain of a ship using his sextant, or the yearly ceremony at the Cenotaph, it would have been to them "sun-worship" and "stone-worship."

ORIENTATION

In other districts it is a frequent experience to find churches oriented to the same angle as the trackway which is alined through them.

To follow up this aspect, either all the six-inch Ordnance maps must be consulted, or original observations made at the churches. I am unable to take either of these courses before publishing this book. I have only seen the two six-inch sheets for most of Cambridge Borough.

In these I note that both Great St. Mary's and St. Clement's churches are oriented to the tracks (for sunrise at the Equinoxes and at Midsummer respectively) coming through them.

It is most probable that there are other instances to be found in the larger district I cover.

The popular idea that churches are oriented to sunrise on the festival day of the saints to which they are dedicated is not confirmed by evidence. See again *Byways in British Archæology*.

I see much general evidence that the custom or practice of orientation to sunrise commenced in pagan times, and that when a pagan site had a Christian edifice built on it the tradition of the old orientation continued.

To some readers the connection between old tracks and sun-observation may seem a fantasy. Note, therefore, the following definitions from Pughe's Welsh Dictionary:

—

Llwybr = "A path, a track."
Llwybro = "To go a course, to travel."
Gole = "Light, splendour."
Wybwr = "An aerologist, an astronomer."

While there follows the omnibus word revealing track-making by Celtic astronomers or science-men.

Golwybro = "To make a slight track or path."

SEASONAL PLACE-NAMES

It is easy for bookish wisdom to pour scorn on surface meanings or surmises regarding place-names. Nevertheless a neglect of the obvious sometimes leads to true ignorance of facts. For example, I know one Gloucestershire man, who having found traces of one Huguenot glass-furnace, proceeded to identify and find actual remains of early glass-making on about four unsuspected sites, by the simple expedient of hunting up farms on the map named Glasshouse.

Only last December the owner of a farm near Ledbury brought to me samples of pottery-shards found in digging a culvert. They had obviously a classic outline —Romano-British—this afterwards confirmed.

I asked him if the fields had any place-names. He replied that it had only been enclosed early in the 19th century, but that the site was on a bit of common land which gave name to the adjoining farm—JUGS GREEN.

Here the fact of a pottery had been preserved in a name all down the centuries (for no pottery later than say the fifth century was found), but no antiquary had woke up to the meaning of the name.

It was the name "Noon's Folly"—in two places—that revealed to me first the mid-day sighting lines detailed in the next chapter.

There is another Folly Hill, evidently a sighting point, above Newmarket, whether with its associated tree-clump, I know not.

Helion Moat embodies the Greek word for sun. The same root comes through Celtic tongues, in many place-names, for *heul* is ancient Welsh and also Cornish for sun, which is *haul* in modern Welsh.

So we get Hellesbury Beacon in Cornwall, Hellstone (a cromlech in Dorset), Helman Tor (E. Cornwall), and helen in other names. I shall mention how this *Helion* moat with its northern alinement caused me to look up the Herefordshire place with name alike, and sure enough an unmistakable northern line came through this.

Hunting out the "North" and "South" places in the

Cambridge map gave me alinements 26 and 31, not depending solely on the "North" names on each, but on other sighting points and fragments of track.

The Herefordshire eastern alinement I have given goes over the apex of *East*nor Hill, in which parish the map also reveals other names denoting seasonal sighting, namely:—May Hill, New Year's Wood, Midsummer Hill, Evendine, Winter Coomb, Beacon Farm, and Gold Hill. The last, dropping the intrusive "d," reveals the Celtic "gole" for light, the same element occurring in the Cambridge Goldstones, a spot which two tracks are sighted through. It may turn out that the Cambridge 6-inch maps will prove to be a happy hunting ground for such seasonal names.

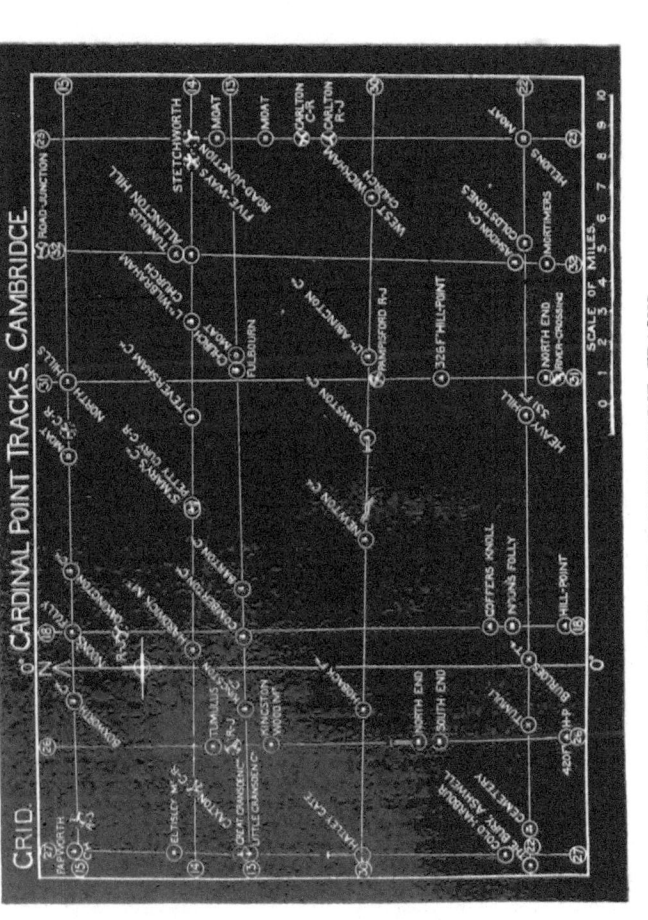

PLAN V.   GRID OF CARDINAL-POINT TRACKS.

7
CARDINAL-POINT ALINEMENTS

We are all familiar with the arrow and its cross-bar so essential to all maps to indicate the axis of the world's rotation, that is, the true north. Surely this precise direction and its record must have been equally essential to the science-men of old? One association of such men (I am not enquiring whether these were the ones who made the alinements in my maps), had, according to Julius Cæsar, "many discussions as touching the stars and their movements, the size of the universe and of the earth, the order of nature"—"they do not think it proper to commit these utterances to writing, although in almost all other matters they make use of Greek letters." If not in writing, why not recorded on the land itself?, especially as all traditions of this particular sect connect them with out-door ritual, done "in the eye of the sun."

Another indicating clue (not followed up in this district), is given by *Aegelnoth's Stone*, where, according to a record in Hereford Cathedral Library, a Shire-mote met in the reign of Cnut. Canon Bannister, in his *Place-names of Herefordshire*, under "Aylestone Hill, Hereford," quotes it as being *Aegelnothes stan* ante 1038 (Kemble), and remarks: "*Aegilnoth* or *Aegil* is the sun-archer of Teutonic mythology," but proceeds (as is a passing custom of place-name experts), to assign the name to "a prosaic English settler." But it is strange that according to the English Place-name Societies volume of Buckinghamshire, not only does Aylesbury contain this same name of *Aegil*, but it is found also in Aylesworth (Nth.), Aylesford (K.), Aylesbeare (D.), and Aylestone (L.)

I surmise that another Aegil-stone is to be found in the AGGLESTONE standing on a mound at Studland Heath, Dorset. This is illustrated and described in Mr. W. Johnson's *Byways in British Archæology*; he notes that "much pagan tradition is associated with this block," and ascribes some "rock-basins" on it to natural agencies. It has the position and appearance of a mark-stone, and it seems possible that the hollows were for beacon-fires.

Frankly, until I was well on with the task of the Cambridge map-work, I did not suspect that these early science-surveyors, as well as making purely travel alinement, had laid down on the land the sun-archer's direction-arrow, north and south.

A place-name revealed it. Two miles east of Royston is Noon's Folly Farm; the "Folly" indicating a sighting point on a track, and the "Noon" element suggesting that this track might be a seasonal or meridional one. Searching the map for other seasonal names, I found—14½ miles away—another Noon Folly Farm. It was almost precisely north of the first one. But the line between just missed the tree-clad Goffer's Knoll, with a tumulus on its apex. However, one-eighth mile west of the lower farm, is a point or clump on the map, which I think to be the true Noon's Folly, and the line (No. 18) going through this to the Upper Folly is one degree only east of north.

This led me to investigate an east and west alinement through Great St. Mary's Church, for which I had seen some evidence. This is No. 14, and goes through a circular pre-historic hill enclosure, Allington Hill, St. Mary's being also oriented on the line.

Discoveries of more and more cardinal point alinements on this map then came fast. Place-names called attention to No. 15 (east and west through the Upper Noon's Folly), to No. 25 (with a moat called Helions, the Greek sun-name, on it), to No. 26 (with a North End and a South End place on it), to No. 31 (with a North End and a North Hills).

Seeing actual straight tracks on the map running north and south called my attention to Nos. 25, 26, and 27; also fragments east and west to No. 30.

I make no attempt to surmise "how it was done," but point out that to find true north by an observation of greatest altitude of mid-day sun at certain seasons does not involve (as does sunrise or sunset observation) the serious complication of differences of horizon elevation due to hills, and therefore the north might have been found first, and a right-angle to this then laid out for east and west. A Polar-star observation would be another way.

I found six northern and five eastern alinements on this map, and give them in Plan V. Some little variation from the true axis would be expected. But there is not more than 1 1/8 degree from present true orientation in the northern ones.

The surmise of being made in pairs has evidence in that pairs almost exactly at right angles to each other are there on my diagram, which is not a mere sketch but accurately giving the bearings. The cardinal-point alinements I have since found in other districts are also in similar pairs.

Definite evidence will be seen by surviving lengths of roads on the Ordnance map in the cases of 25, 26, 27, and 30, that these alinements were used for actual tracks.

All these cardinal-point alinements are also marked on Plan II., and details of each one are given in Chapter IV.

The amount by which each line departs from the true cardinal-point is given in figures in Appendix B.

A remarkable feature is that each northern line has a counterpart in one of the eastern lines within half a degree from being at right angles to it, and one pair (26 and 13), has an exact right-angle relation. The table below shows this:

- Nos. 27 and 30 are 17/40ths degree from 90°, and cross at Hatley Gate.
- Nos. 26 and 13 are *exactly* at right angles.
- Nos. 25 and 14 are 9/20ths degree from 90°, and cross at Stetchworth.
- Nos. 31 and 22 are ¼ degree from 90°.
- Nos. 18 and 15 are 1/5 degree from 90°, and cross at the Upper Noon's Folly.
- Nos. 32 and 30 are ½ degree from 90°.

The above figures seem to me to indicate that these alinements were made in pairs, probably the Polar one first and the Equinoctial one made to it by some appliance for sighting, giving a right-angle, like the Roman Groma.

It happens that the meridian of Greenwich (0° Longitude), now adopted as the standard for time-keeping throughout the world, passes through this map, and I have imposed in Plans II., III., and V. the north and south indicating-arrow on it, with the east and west bar at right angles.

The striking grid of cardinal-point alinements, which I illustrate separately in Plan V., has some aspects which to me have been unexpected. There is a certain uniformity between the spacing of the N. and S. alinements, but not between the E. and W.

Nos. 27 and 26 are 3.6 miles apart, at middle of map.
Nos. 26 ,, 18 ,, 3.65 ,, ,, ,, ,,
Nos. 18 ,, 31 ,, 8 ,, ,, ,, ,,
Nos. 31 ,, 32 ,, 3.95 ,, ,, ,, ,,
Nos. 32 ,, 25 ,, 3.9 ,, ,, ,, ,,

23.1 miles (checked by the total distance).

The average of the above total, divided by six spaces, is 3.85 miles; it will be seen that the actual spaces on the map differ but little from this, and it looks as if this was intentional. The space between Nos. 18 and 31 is, of course, a double one, in which I do not happen to have found or marked the missing alinement. To be more precise, I found one which, although true N., had its chief mark-points in the Ely map. To find it, take a line from North Hill (5 miles north of Cottenham) and Cottenham Moat in the Ely map, down through the heart of Cambridge to Stone Hill and a moat at Elmdon. It probably picks up old sites at Emanuel and Jesus Colleges, but here my local knowledge is insufficient.

It seems probable that there are six corresponding east and west alinements in this map in place of the five which I have found.

There is NOT THE SAME UNIFORMITY of spacing in these equinoctial lines.

Nos. 15 and 14 are 4.1 miles apart, at middle of map.
Nos. 14 ,, 13 ,, 1.5 ,, ,, ,, ,,
Nos. 13 ,, 30 ,, 4.3 ,, ,, ,, ,,
Nos. 30 ,, 22 ,, 5.3 ,, ,, ,, ,,

———
15.2 miles (checked by the total distance).
———

The average of above total, divided by four spaces, is 3.8 miles. This is a curiously near figure to the average of the north and south lines. The ACTUAL spacing, however, departs widely from this theoretical average.

As I know that some minds will at once jump at a probability of the Romans having done this as part of a systematic land survey into squares, let me mention that these figures do not fit in with Roman miles, nor with the spacing between pairs of north and south lines I have to quote in Herefordshire and Radnorshire, which are 6.1 and 5.45 miles respectively.

My own general view is that a geometric land-survey system is quite incompatible with an alinement system (such as I illustrate), which takes HIGH PLACES as mark-points; and that, although a rough ideal of a fairly uniform distance between these utility cardinal-point lines (laid down for communal information) was attempted, the older plan of hill-points for terminals prevailed.

I should also mention that the above spacing does not accord with the planning of land into "Quintarial limites forming a Possessa (810 acres)" which Sir Montague Sharpe adopts for the plans in his book on *Antiquities of Middlesex* (G. Bell & Sons, London, 1919), these being 1 1/8 inch square.

Moreover, unless the connection between barrows and camps of dates at least as old as the Iron Age is denied to the whole system, there was no sufficient private property in land at the time to make any such system of land-survey useful or likely.

The strange fact that one of the best authenticated N. and S. alinements I know (that in Radnor Forest), goes through a CUP-MARKED stone, which also seems to have cardinal-point alinements in its cups, precludes, I think, a Roman origin for what I demonstrate.

CARDINAL-POINT TRACKS IN THE WEST

Although this book deals with Cambridge local tracks, it is not out of place to strengthen the case newly presented in this chapter with similar instances I now find round my own neighbourhood, in places which I have visited and explored for years past.

One find came through following up the *Helions* name. Near Much Marcle, Herefordshire, is an ancient manor-house now called Hellens, but Heliun in 1287, and Helyon in 1394. 45 years ago, when making a survey of Herefordshire Dovecotes, I photographed there the fine memorial one, dated 1642. To be brief the following north and south alinement comes down through it. Bishops Frome Church—Kingston Bridge (present River Frome crossing)—Munsley moated mound—Pixley Church—Hellens—Linton Church—Burton Manor. Crossing this is the Ledbury Church Lane alinement, which I photographed for my first trackway-book. It goes through Putley Church—edge of Aylton Churchyard—Putson (homestead)—Church Lane—Tower of Ledbury Church—Deadman's Thorn—Eastnor Hill (highest point)—Northern vallum of Midsummer Hill Camp.

The reality of this as a trackway is confirmed by the skilled excavations made at Midsummer Hill Camp by Mr. I. I. Hughes, F.R.G.S., who found in the northern ditch an unusual feature, two paved ways of different dates, one a foot below the other. He makes a surmise "That the ditch may have been used at some time or times as a track." Mr. Hughes did not know of my work, but the paved way he found is exactly at the spot where the above alinement crosses the Malvern Ridge, and in the same direction. He dates the Camp to be about, the Iron Age, and therefore the paved way must be as old or older. Details and plans of this in the *Woolhope Club Transactions* for 1924.

A CUP-HOLLOW STONE AS CARDINAL-POINT RECORD

(Figs. VI., VII. and VIII.)

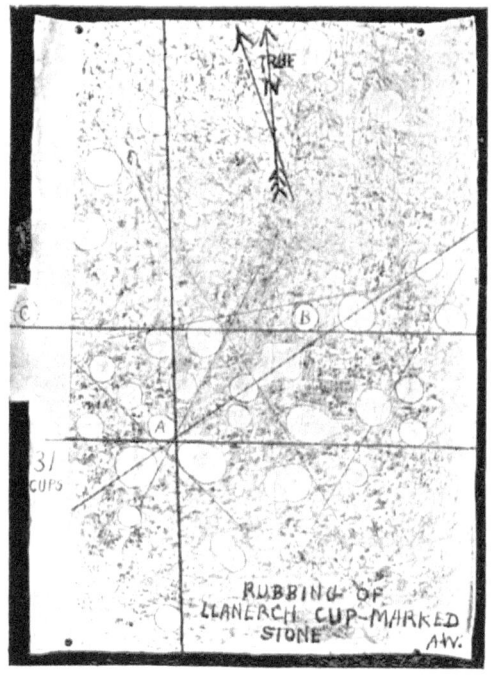

Fig. VI.
A rubbing of the cup-mark stone, Llanerch Farm, Radnor Forest.

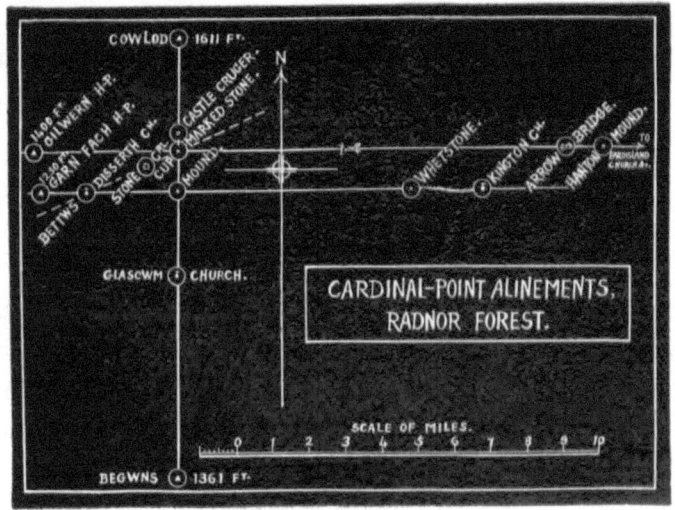

PLAN VII.
Cardinal-point tracks through the Llanerch stone, and other mark points.

Dr. Graves, Bishop of Limerick, many years ago called attention to the frequent cases of alinement which he noted on Irish cup-marked stones. He ventured the opinion that they were a kind of rough diagram of the raths or mounds in the district, which he also found to aline in threes.

I have little personal knowledge of such stones, one in the Grimsel Valley, Switzerland, and the one I shall now mention, being the only ones I have seen or photographed. However, I find almost half of those illustrated in books (as Sir Jas. Simpson's), show evidence of such alinement, and I illustrate and call attention to the fact in the *Ley Hunter's Manual*.

I now see a striking connection between a cup-marked

stone I know well, and a north and south alinement also well known, visited and photographed. I must give it briefly, but the whole subject requires detailed treatment beyond space available here. It is in the Radnor Forest district.

Following a visit by the Woolhope Club in 1928 to that fine mound on Radnor Forest—Cruger Castle— (illustrated in *The Old Straight Track*), a fellow member (Mr. Walter Pritchard), working on alinements, discovered a fine cup-marked stone, at Llanerch Farm, a little south of the mound. I visited and photographed the stone the same year, and took a rubbing of the cup-marks on it, also taking as careful a bearing as possible, and marking it on the paper while on the stone. I also (as soon as I got home) tested for alinements, and inked in those of four cups which I found, as I considered lines of three to be of no value as proof. I could not at that time see any tangible proof of anything, and put it down to this (broken) stone having probably been moved. The reproduction I give is of this crude rubbing exactly as I finished it (outlining then the rather indefinite edges of the cups) in 1928, the magnetic and true bearings being then marked. I found, soon after, a north and south alinement through Cruger Castle and other good mark-points.

It was not until this present work on Cambridge maps began that I saw that this cardinal-point alinement actually went exactly through the cup-marked stone, that there were two or more east-and-west alinements crossing, just as I found about Cambridge, and, above all, that the lines which three years ago I had marked on this rubbing, DO CRUDELY REPRESENT ONE NORTH AND

SOUTH AND TWO EAST AND WEST ALINEMENTS in connection with the cups. It seems to me good evidence of a pre-historic map-record.

In pre-historic times, where three or more circles (whether of earthen banks, stone-circles, or cup-hollows) aline, the basis of alinement is usually to the edge of the circle, that is, when the circles are the same size -they also aline by their centres, but not when they are of uneven size. Striking evidence of this will be found in the diagrams of The Hurlers (Cornwall), and similar circles at Stanton Drew (Somerset), given by the late Hadrian Allcroft in Vol. I., *The Circle and the Cross*, p. 250. The same fact can be traced in Figs. 41 and 47 in Lockyer's Stonehenge, and this is why the lines in Fig. VI. are to the edges of the cups.

A Glasgow archæologist, Mr. Ludovic M. Mann, in his book *Archaic Sculpturings* (W. Hodge and Co., Edinburgh and London, 1915), detects an astronomical purpose in such stones in Scotland. He finds alinements through both the centres and the edges of the cups, and says: "We are apparently now on the verge of obtaining a clear conception of how pre-historic man worked to get his cardinal and solstitial points fixed, and what he understood of the movements of the heavenly bodies." He goes on: "The apparently isolated cairns, the groups of standing stones far distant from each other, and the detached sets of rock carvings well removed from each other, may all form part of one widely spread design; and the surveyor of pre-historic monuments should endeavour to show this relationship in his charts."

Fig. VIII.   CUP-MARK STONE, LLANERCH FARM.

THE CARDINAL POINT ALINEMENTS IN RADNOR FOREST

a. N. and S.—½ degree from true. Cowlod Hill, 1,611 feet—Cruger Castle Mound—Cup-marked stone at Llanerch Farm—Mound (locally called the Four Stones) —Glascwm Church—The Begwns (Beacon) hill point, 1,361 feet.

b. W. and E.—½ degree. Circular 1,400 feet contour hill-point on Gilwern Hill—Cup-mark stone—1/3 mile of road near Yardro—Moated Mound near Hanton, Titley —Eardisland Church—Farm called Cornhill Cop— Caswell Moat in Leominster—Eaton Bridge crossing of Lugg. A long-distance line.

c. W. and E. exact. Garn Fach, 1,250 hill-point—Bettws Disserth   Church—Mound   (Four   Stones)—The

Whetstone on Hargest Ridge—On 12 miles on mountain road—Kington Church.

B. is minus one degree from being at right angles to the Begwns—Cowlod line. C. is half a degree short.

These three land alinements comprise a meridian line over good mark-points with two equinoctial lines crossing at two of the mark-points, one being the cup-mark stone.

Refer to Fig. VI., untouched from when done three years ago, when I had no ideas about archaic cardinal points, and lines apparently representing (if crudely) these three lines will be seen. Is it an archaic diagram? The angle is not an accurate right-angle, but then the stone has a rounded, not a flat, surface. Dr. Wheeler gives only four cup-marked stones in all Wales, this being a fifth, so there is little room for accidental coincidence in these cardinal-point alinements passing through it.

Two other good east and west alinements pass through this northern track. They start from hill-points—Little Hill and Wylfre respectively, and a mark-point on the first is Turret Mound in Hell Wood, and on the other Hell Moat in Sarnsfield Coppice. Compare the "Helion" names.

All this ground is very familiar to me. I have visited half of the points named, and photographed many of them.

Note how in the cup-hollow alinements shown on page 20 of the *Ley Hunter's Manual* there are again examples of lines at right angles. There three alining cups are accepted, as the total number present is only ten. But with the thirty-one cups present on the Llanerch stone, alinement of four cups is the minimum accepted.

I find another well-proved north and south line 5.45 miles east of this one, coming down through that "Four Stones" near Walton, illustrated in the *Old Straight Track*. One is also specified in another part of England, at page 224 of the same book.

8
PLACE-NAMES

Just to glance at some not seasonal, but perhaps connected with tracks. First, the quaint ones, the reproach in Thistley Grounds Farm, the mystery in Mobs Hole and Moco. Are Munseys, Money Hill, and The Moon all on Moon alinements, or what? Dumpilow Farm indicates a tumulus, which once "humpty" was also "dumpty"—low and flat. It had probably been levelled, and if so all the King's horses and all the King's men can't replace it. Why Wrangling Corner? I only know that a track unexpectedly came to it.

Jack-o'-Thumb's Farm seems to link up with track-making; all the Jacks of legend were clever mechanical blades, and I find in other districts a Jack's Green, and a Climbing Jack's Common, both high up of mountain sides.

There are two "Low" Farms, and many "Low" names, as Shardeloes (mound with pottery shards), Mutlow (the mound which was also a moot or folk-assembly place), Limlow Hill, with a tumulus, Burloes, where ancient burials were found on this hill-top farm, and Bobloes.

There is a Howe Wood, a Howe House, and a How Farm, but this corruption of the Saxon "hlaew" is not so common here as the other corruption "low."

The Great Covens Wood (Weston Colville), with its moat, should be investigated, as a "Coven" was a gathering of witches.

There are two Arbury earthworks. A "bury" was always an earthwork first, even if a town afterwards. And "Ar"? Might it not be a dropping of the "H" in " Har," ancient.

Cold Harbour places—the subject of perennial discussions—number two in this map. My tracks go through both—they always are on such tracks. Major Dunning, in his *Roman Road to Portslade*, not knowing of my thesis, reports his surprise to find that four Cold Harbour places in Sussex lie on one straight line in the map—assuredly here an old straight one.

It is repeatedly stated that all the Cold Harbours are on Roman roads. Not one of the five which I find on this and the adjoining maps is on a through road at all, but is at the end of a farm road leading out of a road not marked "Roman." Like other farms, they are on a *cul de sac*.

I have found seven separate cases in the Place-name books where the earlier forms of such places were "Cole" Harbour. The "d" is a false intrusion, and there is no "chilly" meaning to the word. It is simply a form of the Celtic place-name element "cole," a mutation of "gole-" light, and occurs in names for many farms and hills, usually beacon hills. One has only to look at the many Cold Oaks, Cold Elms, Coldman places, and so on, to know that there is some corruption here; they are not chilly.

The "Gold" names, as Goldstones (there is a Goldstone at Hove), are corrupted forms of "Cole." The Celtic mutation between "c" and "g" is shown in the Pembroke Church, Llangolman, dedicated to St. Colman.

A German calendar describes and illustrates a tall grooved stone like the Yorkshire Devils Arrow, "called Gollen or Colgen stein, regarded by some as a boundary stone or landmark, by some as a menhir used in Celtic worship, and by others as a sign or mark of an ancient seat of justice, or place of execution."

No. 1 track, through Cambridge, comes down through Cold Harbour Farm, and also on part of a footpath through Coldham Common. Eliminate the "d" in both places to get at the meaning. This track also comes through another deceptively named place, Scotland Farm. The late J. G. Wood, F.G.S., in a paper on the numerous "Scot" and "Scotland" places, found that they had nothing whatever to do with the northern nation, but were shelter places for early watchers or scouts.

There are not many of the "Col" or "Cole" places in the Cambridge district. Weston Colville, one of them, perhaps Cowless Hall another.

I do not find "Dod" names, also an attribute of track making. There is a "Tute" Farm, a Celtic name for mound.

"Street" and "Stret" names are plentiful. In one case

(crowded out of my map), I found Silver (Silvia) Street Farm, Streetly End, and Streetly Hall on one alinement with a mile of present-day straight road.

As to tracks to potteries, Crocksford Farm is almost certainly on one, and probably Red Cross—a cross-road spot—as is Mark's Grave, where a suicide has been buried with a stake through his body. Whether this denotes a surname or a mark-stone I cannot say.

There are a few "Salt," "Whit" and "wick" places. I find but one "beacon" name, and that with a well-proved track through it. I am inclined to think that most such names if not on the top of a hill, denote rather a track laid out or marked by a beacon at intervals, than a beacon fire at the site.

9

CONFIRMATION AND MORE TRACKS

After map-evidence (as here given), if field work follows, corroboration on the ground usually comes. Such as finding unrecorded mark-stones, hollow roads, hill-notches. Or sometimes the ghost of a track, seen in pasture land in very dry seasons, or in ripe corn near harvest. I know of little field-work done in this district, but with the first copy of the map sent out, my son, Allen Watkins, relates of a tramp made in the Royston district: "Leaving Strethall Church . . . . . I met a labourer and passed the time of day. I told him my route from Royston, "Ah, you came by the Roman road. Now when I first came to these parts, the older folk said that there did used to be an old Roman road straight from Strethall Church here, towards Cambridge. I've never seen it myself; but when the corn grows, you can see exactly where the old road went, by the poorer crop; I've often seen that." This was a capital piece of confirmation, for the labourer introduced the subject of roads himself; I never said a word about them, and of course the track he saw was the one marked on your map from Cambridge to Strethall Church, No. 4."

A later instance where my son visited two mark-points (on No. 19 track), "Anglesea Abbey" and "The Abbey." They were not marked as ancient on the map, but the line (investigated because Chesterton Road pointed straight at the Castle Mound) came through them. My son reported: That Anglesea Abbey, now a modern house, was founded in 1100 A.D. and there is now a rectilinear moat. The Abbey, by Commercial End (Swaffham), is also old; a house is erected on the old foundations, and a bit of old wall still stands, but that local people were not able to give the origin. The map did not mark these as old, but the alinement managed to find them out.

Queer bits of confirmation often come when plotting out maps. No. 12, for instance, sighted through Great and Little Eversden Churches and The Tower, has a fragment of straight road at Weston Colville, coming out of its way to be on the line, evidently a surviving ancient fragment.

Another type of confirmation: On the adjoining Ely map, a most convincing straight line comes through St. Ives and Holywell Churches, the corner of Cottenham churchyard, a Cold Harbour Farm, and the edge of Soldiers Camp. When this map was joined to the Cambridge one, the alinement continued as the line I have marked dotted in the top right-hand corner of Plan II. (47), coming through Exnal and Burwell Churches, and to a hill-point above Newmarket.

Another such instance was found on the Ely map in the straight ancient "Causeway" seen to be sighted on Henny Hill, and edging (in the usual manner of tracks), the camp-entrenchments of Soldiers Hill. The confirming point about this is that when extended into the next map, I found the line go through Impington and Coton Churches.

It is convenient to label these extra alinements, and I will call the St. Ives No. 47 and the Henny Hill No. 48.

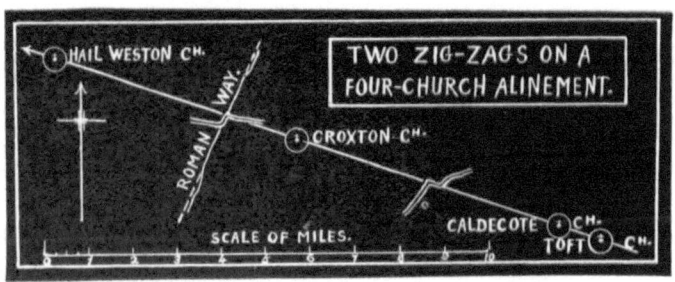

PLAN IX.

I have found that sharp zig-zags in present-day roads are almost always at places where an ancient alined track crosses the other (perhaps more modern). I noted an instance of such a zig-zag near Caxton Church. Extending the "zig," I found it go through Toft, Caldecote and Croxton Churches; on to a point near Winteringham, where a "Roman road"—an alined track, crosses it at another "zig," and on (in the Bedford map) through several corroborations to Hail Weston Church and the Castle Hill and Church at Yelden. This No. 49 (Plan IX.)

No. 50, along the centre of the great avenue of Wimpole, was given in the *Ley Hunter's Manual* by a correspondent, who found it confirmed in an adjoining map. I did not insert it in Plan II. because I did not see the mark-points total up to my 5 as minimum. But I am fairly satisfied that it is an ancient line, as I have found cross-lines (not all fully proved) coming through the Pool, the Mansion, and the Tower. It is well worth following up.

After I had the map quite crowded enough, my eye caught a line of a boundary, a track and Vallance Farm pointing to a church, and it provided the striking confirmation of coming to a point near Barley Church, where two lines already crossed—an evident sighting hill-point. This No. 51 is a good track. Hill-point—Heydon Church—Bit of road—Boundary, track, Tumulus, and Vallance Farm—Great Chesterford Church—Cross-road—Hadstock Church.

Another confirmation, this time verifying the actual alinement of an ancient causeway through church sites, is again in the Ely map. Conybeare's *Rides round Cambridge* mentions the Soham Causeway, made by Harvey de Briton, first Bishop of Ely, and credited with supernatural sanction. St. Edmund appeared in a dream to a man of Exning, instructing him to suggest the causeway to the Bishop. This causeway, part of a main road now, is straight and sighted through Ely Cathedral at one end and Fordham Abbey at the other. It is only about 18 miles from Cambridge. (No. 52).

I will now give a few other alinements, which, like others in this chapter, are not marked on either of my maps. Some of them have the full 5-point proof.

No. 53. Moat at Manor Farm, Great Eversden—Grange Farm, Cambridge—St. Peter's in the Castle Church, Cambridge—Chesterton Moat—Biggin Abbey.

. . .

No. 54. Moat near Hatley—The Tower in Wimpole Avenue—Road-junction near Hauxton—Great Shelford Church—Road-junction, Stapleford—Straight road and field track for 1¼ miles.

No. 55. Moat at Papworth Hall—Knapwell Church—Eye Hall Moated-house—Swaffham Prior Church. (This alinement is parallel to No. 15 less than a mile apart.)

No. 56. Papworth St. Agnes Church—Caxton Pastures Moat—Hoback Farm—A second Hoback Farm, with moat—Tumulus near Melbourn—Heath Farm Moat—Barley Church. (The two Hoback Farms on one line called my attention to this well-proved track, but being so close to another, I had to omit marking it on my map, but its points are ringed).

No. 57. Arbury Camp (corner of)—Donkey's Common, Cambridge—Road-junction, Sawston—The Spike road-junction—Approximately on about three miles of present road to edge of Roman settlement, ICANUM—Great Chesterford Church—Short road at Littlebury.

No. 58. South edge of Arbury Banks (Ashwell)—Goffer's Knoll with tumulus—Road-junction, Coach and Horses

—Cross-roads at Hinxton—Little Linton Moat—West Wickham Church—397 Hill-point.

No. 59. Cross-roads, Royston—On ¾ mile of supposed Icknield Way—Noon's Folly (both Farm and sight-point)—Cross-road and approximately on track for a mile)—Ickleton Church—Haw's Hill, 272 feet.

No. 60. Wiggens Green—Wigmore Pond—Goldstones—(Byrds Homestead)—Road-junction—Littlebury Church—Cross-road near Calmere End.

No. 61. Tumulus north of Sturmer Hall—Wiggens Green—Helion Bumpstead Church—Helion Moat—Road-junction and bit of road.

I add these alinements (too many, some will say), not marked on my maps, because some local investigators might find real information in them. Some are quite as well authenticated as those marked. No. 60 is given as having two "Wig" names on it. "Wig" might be Saxon for war, or a corruption of "Weg"—a road.

PROOF OF AN ANCIENT INSTINCT

Mr. N. Woodhead, M.Sc., of Bangor University, remarks in the notebook of the Straight Track Club: "We well suppose that the ancient folk had this faculty (sense of direction) well-developed. My brother and I have tested ourselves, and find we can keep to a straight course for five miles, and reach a point within 20 yards of our original objective. We have repeated the experiment many times within the last five years. On one occasion my brother and I were leading a party of scouts to the summit of a mountain which was four miles distant. We saw the peak from our base. I led straight for it, the boys following in file and my brother bringing up the rear. A thick sea mist blotted out our objective, which was completely invisible for three-quarters of an hour, and I had no track or intermediate points to guide me. But I held on my way over heather, gorse and rock, making occasional twists to dodge the more unpleasant gorse-bushes. When the summit cairn (Caer Tre'r Ceiri) loomed through the mist, I stopped and noted with satisfaction that my party was alined on to it."

10
NOTES

MAPS

One is absolutely necessary to tramp the alinements. And that one MUST be a one-inch Ordnance sheet. The half-inch or quarter-inch maps as used for motorists are quite useless, as they have not the details required. In fact for villages or towns it is difficult to do without consulting the six-inch maps.

The POPULAR folding map (Cambridge), No. 85, at 2/6, conforms in area to my Plans II. and V., so do not accept the 3/- "Cambridge District" map, which is poorer value, and does not conform.

BOOKS

Ancient Mark-Stones of East Anglia (W. A. Dutt, Flood and Son, Lowestoft, 2/-). This by one who has confirmed by field-work the pre-Roman. sighted tracks, and it throws light on the system.

Stonehenge. (Sir Norman Lockyer, Macmillan, 12/6.) Details the pioneer work of this skilled astronomer in finding sun-alinements in most of the British megalithic monuments.

Either *The Ley Hunter's Manual* (2/-) or *The Old Straight Track* (18/-), my own text-books, which are detailed in a page after the index. The first-named the most recent, and it has fresh matter on camps.

Archæology of the Cambridge Region. (Dr. Cyril Fox, Cambridge University Press, 31/6.) Indispensable, being crammed with reliable topographical facts detailed by a brilliant expert, and dating, where possible, the many finds and "monuments."

DR. CYRIL FOX'S BOOK

Cambridge is exceptionally fortunate in this skilled compendium of the local knowledge bearing on my theme. I, therefore, glance at several points, noting first that I had finished both maps and text in these covers before I saw Dr. Fox's book, and have not altered, omitted, or added anything to my own personal observations in consequence.

The book is absolutely necessary to the real investigator. The author naturally adopts the orthodox opinion (I think, wrongly), that straightness and alinement is an exclusive sign of Roman engineering, all earlier ones being sinuous. This excepted, I find his attitude and information as to pre-historic tracks and their mark-points amazingly full, up-to-date, and open-minded. Contrary to many stiff-back authorities, he notes the abundance and importance of pre-Roman tracks other than ridgeways. For instance, p. 156, "The whole area is so seamed with tracks new and old, that accurate determination of a prehistoric route is well nigh impossible." Then he notes (p. 320), that "the Romans are seen to have made extensive use of these earlier ways"; and p. 219, "Occupied areas had, when the Romans came, a network of reasonably good roads, and these, hardened and straightened in places, became vicinal ways, and occasionally, it would seem, main roads."

Ermine Street, Dr. Fox, I gather, classifies as pre-Roman, yet referring (p. 164), to its "Distinctive Roman method of setting out. Great stretches are laid out on the same alignment, changes in direction coinciding with hillcrests."

There is an interesting note on p. 30 concerning upland barrows (these in commanding positions are, I think, so placed for sight-marks), " Our Bronze Age Barrows are all bowl-shaped. They are here, as in similar districts in England, confined almost entirely to the uplands. No primary interment of Roman date in an upland barrow is known to me."

Dr. Fox gives routes for several surmised pre-Roman trackways, and it will be interesting to compare these with mine.

The orthodox dictum that the mounds on which Norman keeps have been built must always be classified as "Norman Mottes" and dated for that period, seems to be completely thrown over by Dr. Fox as regards that of Cambridge Castle, for he treats it as a mound to which the Romans alined their tracks, both in his sketch map on

p. 246; and on p. 166, speaking of Roman roads: "On a clear day one may see how the alignment on Castle Hill, Cambridge, was taken from Fox Hill north of Orwell. The road coincides with a straight line joining the two points." This, by the way, I make to be a good alined track, through Barton Church and several moats as markpoints, lying on the stretch of road seen, and another bit further on.

While I noted an apparent absence of "*Dod*" names in this map, Dr. Fox supplies the deficiency in noting near Barton a Deadman's Way, and a Deadman's Hill. This name always originates from the "Dod," "Did," or "Dud" element.

A most interesting fact, perhaps, bearing on my cardinal-point track alinements, is brought out (p. 199). "The fact that the Bartlow tumuli lie in exact lines north and south conforms to ancient custom, the Chronicle Hills (tumuli) at Triplow having been, in the Early Iron Age, so aligned." Dr. Fox mentions two other groups of tumuli so alined north and south, namely (p. 197), Six Hills Stevenage, and (p. 193) at Rougham, east of Bury St. Edmunds. Three of these groups he puts down as probably Roman.

ALINEMENT

For spelling this word I now follow the New English Dictionary: "The English form, *alinement*, is preferable to *alignment*, a bad spelling of the French." In the Herefordshire village, Linton, is a road called "The Line," which follows a straight sighted track, well confirmed between hill-points, and passing through a "Lynders Wood." A few miles away is a house called "The Lea Line." Through Linton Church (Cambridgeshire) I find three alinements.

BOOK PROPORTION

This book is King Octavo, using an ideal paper size (17 x 24), which has the only proportion (1 to the square-root of 2; the diagonal of a square to its side; or 1 to 1.414) which remains unaltered in proportion in folding down through folio, quarto, and octavo. Its handsome proportion was known and used by early printers.

THE SPADE

This, I think, is the future means for proof of the reality of alined tracks where mark-points indicate them to be. I have done no work on this, but in several cases have seen in sewer and other cuttings such proof where I had, beforehand, surmised tracks to be. It might be but a small indication, where, not being through a wet place, the track was not stoned. Depth I find to be from 18 to 30 inches underground, possibly deeper in places, or less in uplands.

AEROPLANE PHOTOGRAPHY

I am inclined to think, that however valuable this method will be for fairly recent (as mediæval) tracks, and for the heavily stoned Roman roads, it may fail to show the lighter and older tracks, two feet below the surface. Consider that this method succeeds in recording otherwise unseen tracks by only two methods: (*a*), by registering when side-lighted very slight hollows. (*b*), by the differences in colour or growth of surface vegetation caused by a layer of stoned road below the surface. I do not think that the oldest tracks, two feet below ground, show the faintest hollow above it. And when, as usual, they are not stoned, I cannot see how they will affect surface growth.

It jars on one who has copiously photographed illustration for many books, to issue this one with maps and plans only. It is half-a-century since I first provided the illustrations to a book by my field photography. The probable two years' delay needed to follow my custom I cannot face this evening time. So, end this book I must, as I began, incomplete in full proof, with field work lacking as yet. Will the reader who starts on it gladden the heart of an old scout with a note on his finds?

Adventure lies lurking in these lines where I point the way for younger feet than mine. Detective work of sorts; unnoticed mark-stones almost buried in the banks of cross-roads, in the field, or on a town pavement; the edges of an unrecorded camp; a faint mound almost levelled; or, again on the ley of the land, as the eye looks straight on, the point of a distant beacon-hill as a mark on the sky-line.

Who will strike the trail?

APPENDIX A
TABLE OF AZIMUTHS

AZIMUTHS OF APPARENT SUNRISE AND SUNSET FOR LATITUDE OF CAMBRIDGE, 50°.13′. N. Calculated by Rear-Admiral Boyle Somerville, C.M.G., F.S.A.

Elevation of the Horizon.		0°	1°	2°	3°	4°	5°
Summer Solstitial	Sunrise	48°.30′	50°.26′	52°.15′	53°.57′	55°.32′	57°.04′
" "	Sunset	311°.30′	309°.34′	307°.45′	306°.03′	304°.28′	302°.56′
" Bealtaine " (May 6-7)	Sunrise	61°.27′	63°.16′	64°.49′	66°.19′	67°.43′	69°.08′
" "	Sunset	298°.33′	296°.44′	295°.11′	293°.41′	292°.17′	290°.52′
Equinoxes	Sunrise	89°.16′	90°.47′	92°.12′	93°.34′	94°.55′	96°.16′
"	Sunset	270°.44′	269°.13′	267°.48′	266°.26′	265°.05′	263°.44′
Samhain (Nov. 8-9)	Sunrise	116°.47′	118°.28′	120°.06′	121°.45′	123°.12′	125°.01′
" "	Sunset	243°.13′	241°.31′	239°.54′	238°.15′	236°.48′	234°.59′
Winter Solstitial	Sunrise	129°.33′	131°.33′	133°.27′	135°.27′	137°.27′	189°.32′
" "	Sunset	230°.27′	228°.27′	226°.33′	224°.33′	222°.34′	220°.28′

"To find the bearing by prismatic compass, at Cambridge, in 1932, add 12° to the above azimuths (sunrise or sunset). Annual change in variation (Cambridge) is −13′(i.e. subtractive) at present."

I am greatly indebted to Admiral Boyle Somerville for this valuable help for local investigation in this district. In giving it, he does not commit himself to any of my suggested conclusions. He adds the following explanation:—

"Remember that the above are *apparent* sunrises and sunsets, that is, they are the positions on the horizon at which the sun is *actually visible*, when rising or setting; and the azimuths are calculated for the *sun's centre*, not for first emergence over the edge of the horizon (as Sir Norman Lockyer calculated, entirely unwarrantably) nor for the moment when it is seen standing entire on the horizon. We do not know which moment was observed by the ancients, and so the fairest thing is to take the mean, *i.e.*, the sun's centre."

APPENDIX B

AZIMUTHS OF ALINEMENTS ON THE MAPS AND PLANS

		AZIMUTHS.					AZIMUTHS.	
No.	1 Angle of	$110\frac{1}{2}°$	or	$290\frac{1}{2}°$	No. 31 Angle of	$0°$	or	$180°$
,,	2 ,,	$129°$	,,	$309°$	,, 32 ,,	$1°$	,,	$181°$
,,	3 ,,	$138\frac{1}{4}°$	,,	$318\frac{1}{4}°$	,, 33 ,,	$70°$	,,	$250°$
,,	4 ,,	$169°$	,,	$319°$	,, 34 ,,	$61°$	,,	$241°$
,,	5 ,,	$27°$	,,	$207°$	,, 35 ,,	$72°$	,,	$252°$
,,	6 ,,	$38°$	,,	$218°$	,, 36 ,,	$127°$	,,	$307°$
,,	7 ,,	$52°$	,,	$232°$	,, 37 ,,	$61°$	,,	$241°$
,,	8 ,,	$62°$	,,	$242°$	,, 38 ,,	$51°$	,,	$231°$
,,	9 ,,	$52°$	,,	$232°$	,, 39 ,,	$35°$	,,	$215°$
,,	10 ,,	$68\frac{1}{4}°$	,,	$248\frac{1}{4}°$	,, 40 ,,	$42°$	,,	$222°$
,,	11 ,,	$67°$	,,	$247°$	,, 41 ,,	$71°$	,,	$251°$
,,	12 ,,	$88°$	,,	$268°$	,, 42 ,,	$156°$	,,	$336°$
,,	13 ,,	$89°$	,,	$269°$	,, 43 ,,	$165°$	,,	$345°$
,,	14 ,,	$90°$	,,	$270°$	,, 44 ,,	$64°$	,,	$244°$
,,	15 ,,	$89°$	,,	$269°$	,, 45 ,,	$57°$	,,	$237°$
,,	16 ,,	$156\frac{1}{4}°$	,,	$336\frac{1}{4}°$	,, 46 ,,	$66°$	,,	$246°$
,,	17 ,,	$111°$	,,	$291°$	,, 47 ,,	$101°$	,,	$281°$
,,	18 ,,	$179°$	,,	$359°$	,, 48 ,,	$43°$	,,	$233°$
,,	19 ,,	$72°$	,,	$252°$	,, 49 ,,	$109°$	,,	$289°$
,,	20 ,,	$66°$	,,	$246°$	,, 50 ,,	$178°$	,,	$358°$
,,	21 ,,	$80\frac{1}{2}°$	,,	$260\frac{1}{2}°$	,, 51 ,,	$71°$	,,	$251°$
,,	22 ,,	$90°$	,,	$270°$	,, 52 ,,	$142°$	,,	$322°$
,,	23 ,,	$122°$	,,	$302°$	,, 53 ,,	$60°$	,,	$240°$
,,	24 ,,	$124°$	,,	$304°$	,, 54 ,,	$93°$	,,	$273°$
,,	25 ,,	$0°$	,,	$180°$	,, 55 ,,	$89°$	,,	$269°$
,,	26 ,,	$179°$	,,	$359°$	,, 56 ,,	$155°$	,,	$335°$
,,	27 ,,	$1°$	,,	$181°$	,, 57 ,,	$165°$	,,	$345°$
,,	28 ,,	$81°$	,,	$261°$	,, 58 ,,	$72°$	,,	$252°$
,,	29 ,,	$52°$	,,	$232°$	,, 59 ,,	$78°$	,,	$258°$
,,	30 ,,	$91\frac{1}{2}°$	,,	$271\frac{1}{2}°$	,, 60 ,,	$81°$	,,	$261°$
					,, 61 ,,	$56°$	,,	$236°$

I do not attempt to give the right astronomical definition of an azimuth. But for its application to this investigation it is the angle which the alinement makes (counting clockwise) to true north.

Herein comes a difficulty. An alinement (as say No. 22), can be looked at from both ends, and looking eastward, that is to sunrise, this one is 90°; while looking westward it is 270°. If actually sighting to sunrise or sunset, as observers have done from ancient stones, &c., you know which of the two angles you are taking, and only one figure is given as the azimuth. But as regards this book I only know the resulting line, and have no idea (it might be found with local observation) in which direction the track or line was first sighted. No. 22, if sighted in one direction, might be to sunrise at the Equinox, at an horizon elevation of about 1°. But it might also be (as can be noted in Appendix A.) sunset at the Equinox at about the same elevation. Admiral Somerville, in drawing up his table, knew of which these directions he speaks, but in the subjoined table, drawn up as an aid to consulting this, I do not know, and am obliged to give both angles, one of course being always half a circle (180°) more than the first.

These angles were taken from a meridional line with a six-inch circular protractor, and are (I trust) within half a degree (or less) of accuracy.

www.ingramcontent.com/pod-product-compliance
Lightning Source LLC
Chambersburg PA
CBHW020105240426
43661CB00002B/38